OUR ENVIRONMENT

Everything You Need to Know

Written by Jacques Pasquet   Illustrated by Yves Dumont

With translation by Shelley Tanaka

OWLKIDS BOOKS

To the children of this Earth
So that they will never forget its beauty — J.P.

To Lucie, so that she may live in a better world.
To Chantal, for her immense support during the creation of this book — Y.D.

The English-language edition of this book was created in consultation with Dr. Virginia Capmourteres, School of Environmental Sciences, University of Guelph.

Originally published as *Notre Environnement* by Éditions de l'Isatis

Owlkids Books acknowledges the financial support of the Canada Council for the Arts, the Ontario Arts Council, the Government of Canada through the Canada Book Fund (CBF) and the Government of Ontario through the Ontario Creates Book Initiative for our publishing activities.

Published in Canada by
Owlkids Books Inc.
1 Eglinton Avenue East
Toronto, ON M4P 3A1

Published in the United States by
Owlkids Books Inc.
1700 Fourth Street
Berkeley, CA 94710

Library of Congress Control Number: 2019947220

Library and Archives Canada Cataloguing in Publication

Title: Our environment : everything you need to know / written by Jacques Pasquet ; illustrated by Yves Dumont ; translated and adapted by Shelley Tanaka.
Other titles: Notre environnement. English
Names: Pasquet, Jacques, 1948- author. | Dumont, Yves, 1974- illustrator. | Tanaka, Shelley, translator.
Description: Translation of: Notre environnement. | Includes bibliographical references and index.
Identifiers: Canadiana 20190137126 | ISBN 9781771473897 (hardcover)
Subjects: LCSH: Ecology—Juvenile literature. | LCSH: Environmental protection—Juvenile literature.
Classification: LCC QH541.14 .P3713 2020 | DDC j577—dc23

ONTARIO ARTS COUNCIL
CONSEIL DES ARTS DE L'ONTARIO
an Ontario government agency
un organisme du gouvernement de l'Ontario

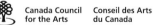
Canada Council
for the Arts
Conseil des Arts
du Canada

Canadä

Manufactured in Guangzhou, Dongguan, China, in September 2019,
by Toppan Leefung Packaging & Printing (Dongguan) Co., Ltd. Job #BAYDC69

A   B   C   D   E   F   G

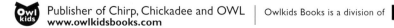
OwlKids Publisher of Chirp, Chickadee and OWL
www.owlkidsbooks.com
| Owlkids Books is a division of  bayard canada

CONTENTS

Bolded words are defined in the glossary.

WHAT EXACTLY IS THE ENVIRONMENT?

The environment is everything around us—from our homes to our streets, neighborhoods, cities, and countries. It's beaches and forests, deserts and oceans. It's the continents we live on; it's our planet Earth. When we talk about the environment, we are usually talking about how healthy—or unhealthy—our planet is.

Our environment includes five essential elements:

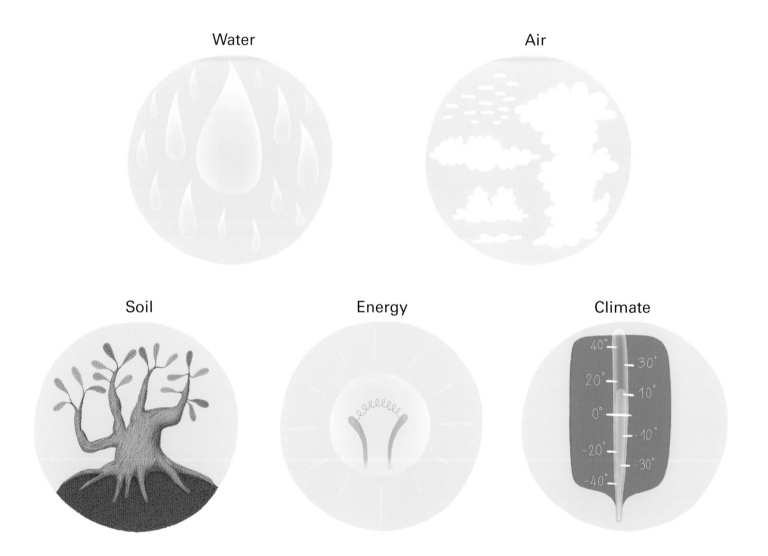

Water

Air

Soil

Energy

Climate

Our environment is constantly being changed by the organisms that live here. We humans, for example, have always tried to improve the conditions we live in. And every change has had an impact on our environment.

For a long time, these changes took place slowly, and nobody worried much about the environment. But then came the **industrial revolution**. People began to build factories to make all the things they wanted. And while industrialization led to rapid changes in science and technology, these factories needed energy to run. Industries and factories have grown, and new communication technologies have emerged. There are also more people in the world, and more of us are living in cities. We need more food, and bigger farms to produce it.

Today, the entire planet is facing the consequences of these changes. The pollution we've generated is contaminating the environment and contributing to **climate change**. That results in rising temperatures and more extreme weather events around the world—more storms, more droughts, more floods.

Protecting our environment—keeping our planet healthy—is an urgent matter. But first, we must know the environment and understand how our way of life has changed it, for good and bad. This will help us take the actions needed for the future health of our planet.

1. WATER

All living things are made mostly of water. Humans are about 60 percent water. Plants are 80 to 85 percent water. And the Earth's surface is 70 percent water. That's why the Earth is called the blue planet.

Where Is the Earth's Water?

About 97 percent of the Earth's water is salt water, which is found mainly in the seas and oceans. It's too salty to drink or use to irrigate crops.

Only 3 percent of the water on Earth is fresh water, so it is a rare and precious thing. We use fresh water to irrigate our farmland and gardens, and we also treat it to make it safe to drink, or **potable**.

There are almost two hundred countries in the world, but nine of them consume more than half of the planet's available fresh water. In the United States and Canada, people use a lot of water in their homes. About 65 percent of that is in the bathroom—for showering, brushing teeth, and flushing the toilet. The remaining 35 percent is used for things like cooking, drinking, and washing clothes. Canadians and Americans use much more water than people in parts of Africa and Asia.

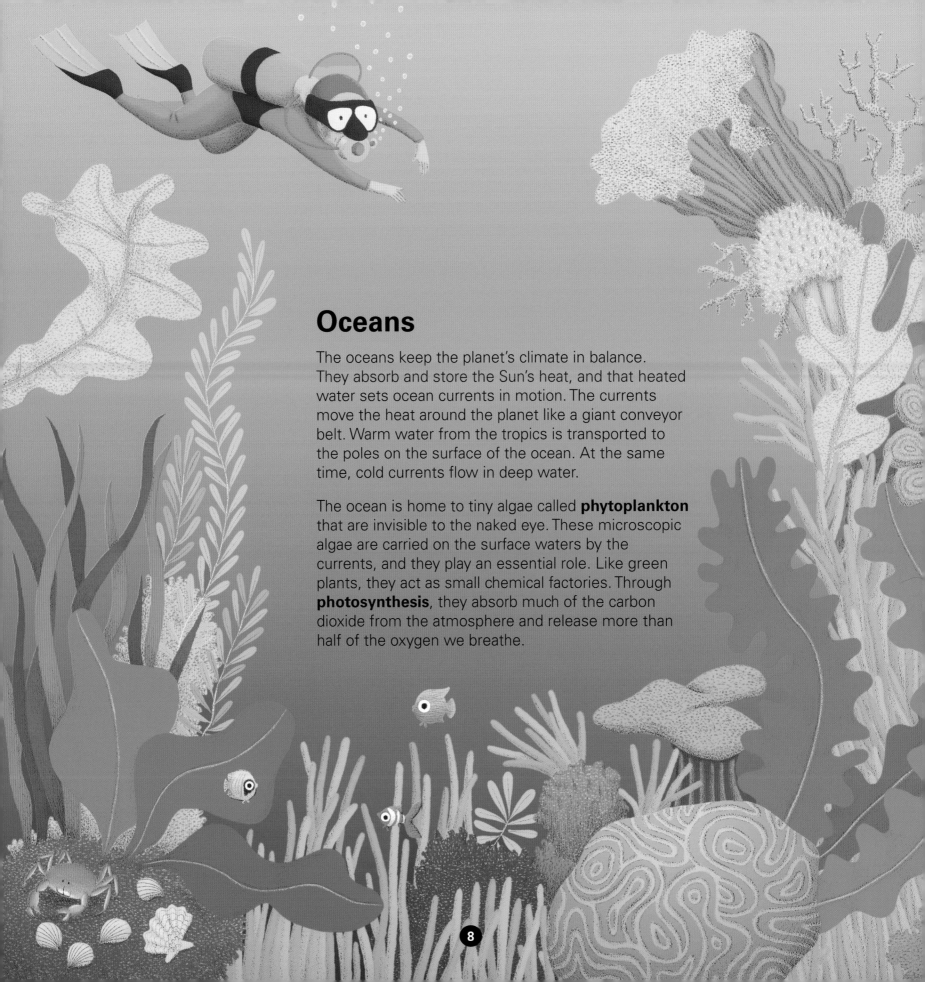

Oceans

The oceans keep the planet's climate in balance. They absorb and store the Sun's heat, and that heated water sets ocean currents in motion. The currents move the heat around the planet like a giant conveyor belt. Warm water from the tropics is transported to the poles on the surface of the ocean. At the same time, cold currents flow in deep water.

The ocean is home to tiny algae called **phytoplankton** that are invisible to the naked eye. These microscopic algae are carried on the surface waters by the currents, and they play an essential role. Like green plants, they act as small chemical factories. Through **photosynthesis**, they absorb much of the carbon dioxide from the atmosphere and release more than half of the oxygen we breathe.

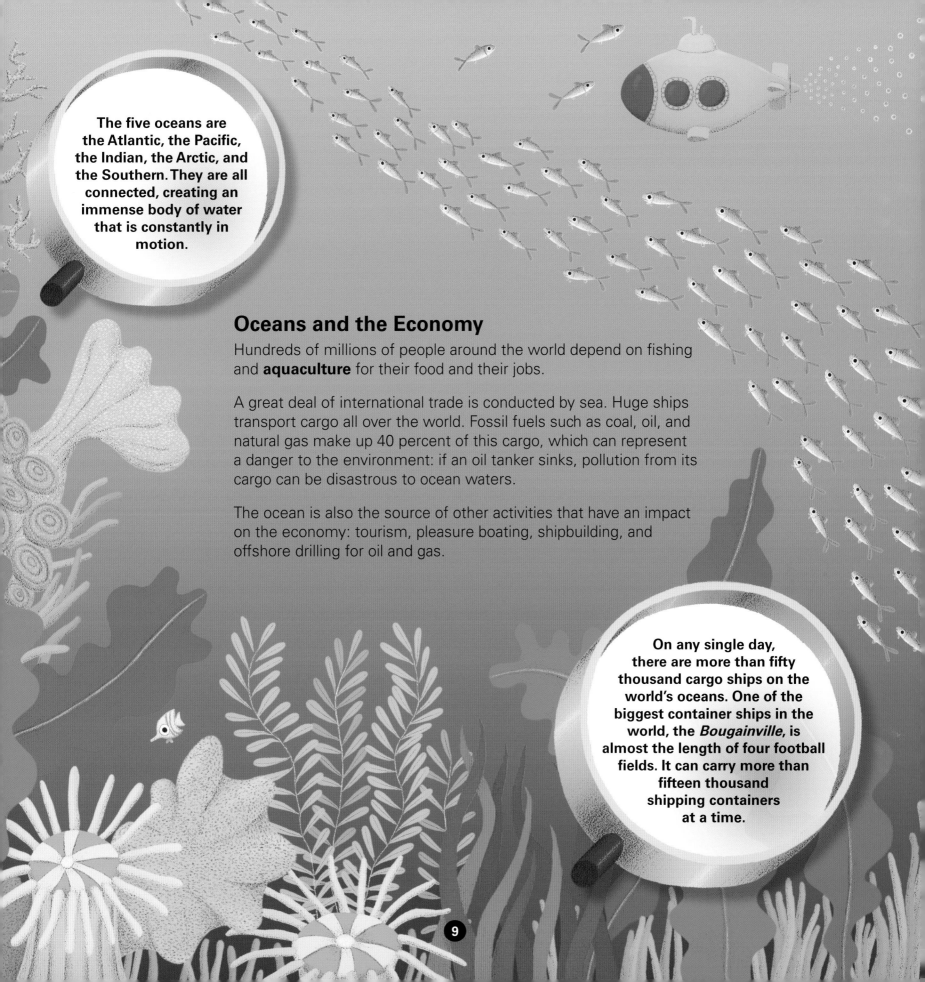

The five oceans are the Atlantic, the Pacific, the Indian, the Arctic, and the Southern. They are all connected, creating an immense body of water that is constantly in motion.

Oceans and the Economy

Hundreds of millions of people around the world depend on fishing and **aquaculture** for their food and their jobs.

A great deal of international trade is conducted by sea. Huge ships transport cargo all over the world. Fossil fuels such as coal, oil, and natural gas make up 40 percent of this cargo, which can represent a danger to the environment: if an oil tanker sinks, pollution from its cargo can be disastrous to ocean waters.

The ocean is also the source of other activities that have an impact on the economy: tourism, pleasure boating, shipbuilding, and offshore drilling for oil and gas.

On any single day, there are more than fifty thousand cargo ships on the world's oceans. One of the biggest container ships in the world, the *Bougainville*, is almost the length of four football fields. It can carry more than fifteen thousand shipping containers at a time.

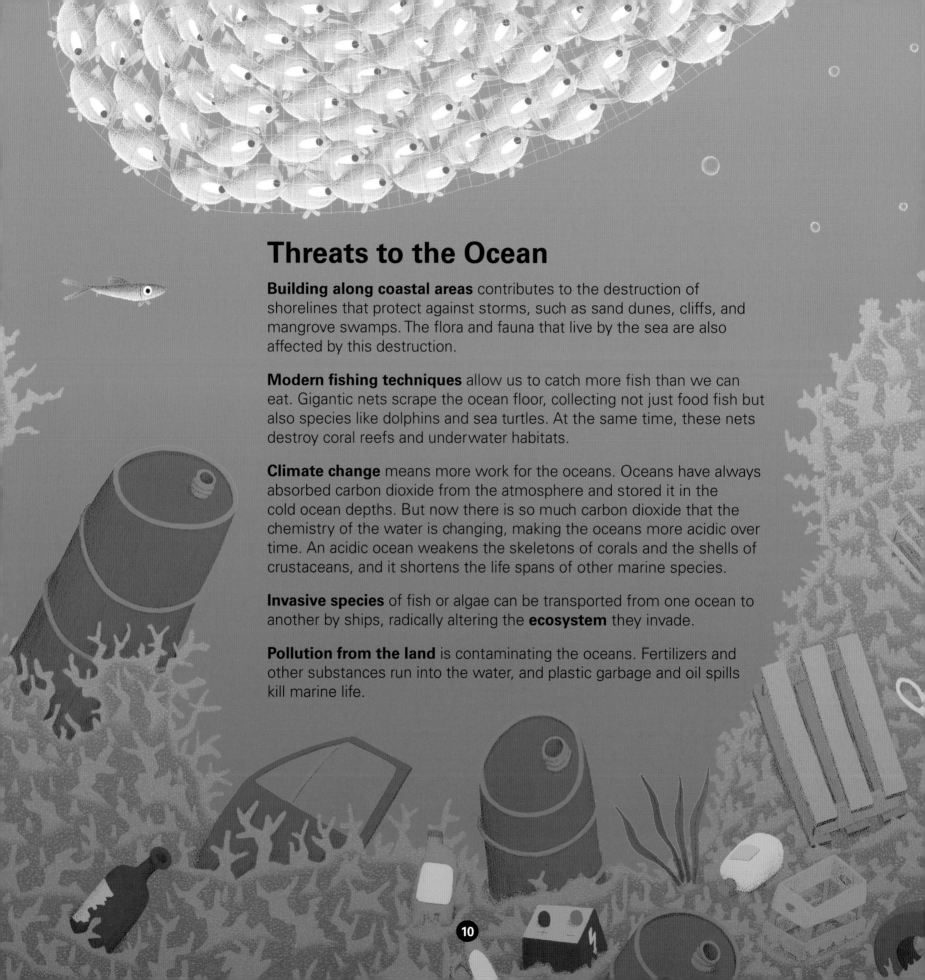

Threats to the Ocean

Building along coastal areas contributes to the destruction of shorelines that protect against storms, such as sand dunes, cliffs, and mangrove swamps. The flora and fauna that live by the sea are also affected by this destruction.

Modern fishing techniques allow us to catch more fish than we can eat. Gigantic nets scrape the ocean floor, collecting not just food fish but also species like dolphins and sea turtles. At the same time, these nets destroy coral reefs and underwater habitats.

Climate change means more work for the oceans. Oceans have always absorbed carbon dioxide from the atmosphere and stored it in the cold ocean depths. But now there is so much carbon dioxide that the chemistry of the water is changing, making the oceans more acidic over time. An acidic ocean weakens the skeletons of corals and the shells of crustaceans, and it shortens the life spans of other marine species.

Invasive species of fish or algae can be transported from one ocean to another by ships, radically altering the **ecosystem** they invade.

Pollution from the land is contaminating the oceans. Fertilizers and other substances run into the water, and plastic garbage and oil spills kill marine life.

The most polluted place in the world is a deserted island in the South Pacific Ocean. Henderson Island is located where several marine currents meet. Researchers have discovered more than thirty-eight million pieces of plastic waste there. Plastic litter in the oceans can damage coral and harm other marine animals that become tangled in garbage or eat small pieces of it.

In the middle of the North Pacific Ocean, there is an island twice the size of Texas made entirely of plastic. This huge whirlpool of waste, called the Great Pacific Garbage Patch, contains an estimated 1.8 trillion pieces of plastic. Other garbage patches are drifting in the North Atlantic, the South Atlantic, and the Western Pacific.

Fresh Water

Seventy percent of the Earth's fresh water is frozen year-round in glacier ice in Antarctica, the Arctic, and various mountain ranges. The other 30 percent amounts to only 0.5 percent of all the water on Earth. It is found mainly in **groundwater**, in lakes and rivers, and in the atmosphere (as water vapor, rain, snow, and clouds).

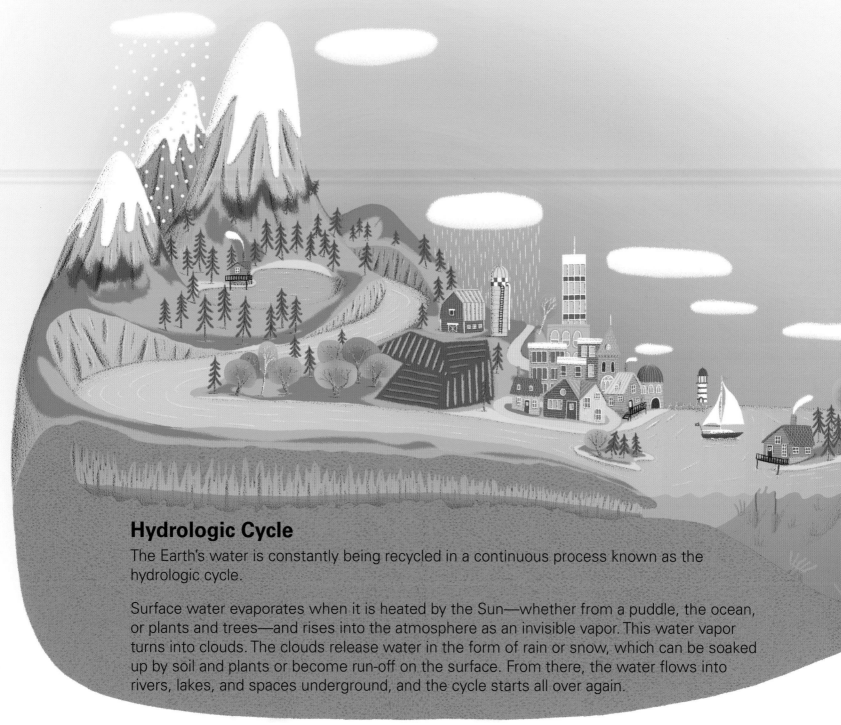

Hydrologic Cycle

The Earth's water is constantly being recycled in a continuous process known as the hydrologic cycle.

Surface water evaporates when it is heated by the Sun—whether from a puddle, the ocean, or plants and trees—and rises into the atmosphere as an invisible vapor. This water vapor turns into clouds. The clouds release water in the form of rain or snow, which can be soaked up by soil and plants or become run-off on the surface. From there, the water flows into rivers, lakes, and spaces underground, and the cycle starts all over again.

Threats to Our Fresh Water

As the world's population grows, there is an increasing demand for water. Can you imagine how much water megacities of the future might need? What would happen if people could not find clean drinking water?

The quality of the world's water is important to all living things. And the risks of water contamination are higher today than they have ever been.

The world's biggest cities:
1. **Tokyo, Japan**
   38 million people
2. **Delhi, India**
   29 million people
3. **Shanghai, China**
   26 million people
4. **São Paulo, Brazil**
   22 million people
5. **Mexico City, Mexico**
   22 million people

Contaminants in Our Fresh Water

These pollutants can be harmful to all living organisms.

- Residues of heavy metals used in industry (mercury, lead, arsenic)

- Chemical fertilizers, pesticides, and **herbicides** used in agriculture and gardening

- Chemicals used to make everyday products, such as household cleaners, shampoos and hand sanitizers, and cosmetics

- Residues from medications

- **Bacteria** from animal and human **excrement**

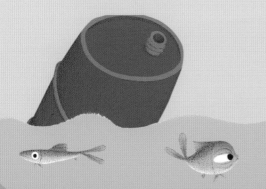

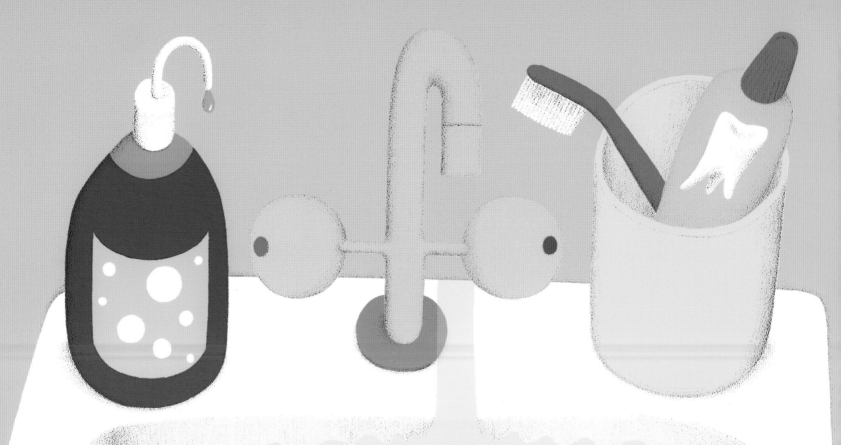

Fresh Water in Our Daily Lives

Everyone uses fresh water—every family, business, and city or town that provides public services such as schools, hospitals, arenas, or parks. We use water to irrigate our crops and feed our livestock (agricultural irrigation accounts for 70 percent of the world's water consumption). And we use water in industry—to produce goods, to cool machinery, and to transport finished products.

At home, most of our water comes out of the tap. We use it to keep ourselves clean, to wash our clothes, to prepare and cook food—and, of course, to drink. And we want it to be of the best possible quality.

Depending on where you live, the water in your home may come from a well, spring, lake, river, or stream. This water can be contaminated because of human activity. Groundwater is particularly sensitive to products used in farming, such as pesticides, fertilizers, and manure. Factories also discharge pollutants into rivers, lakes, and groundwater.

Drinking Water

Since water can be contaminated at its source, it must be treated to make it safe to drink. So pipes carry a community's water to filtration plants, where it's put through several steps:

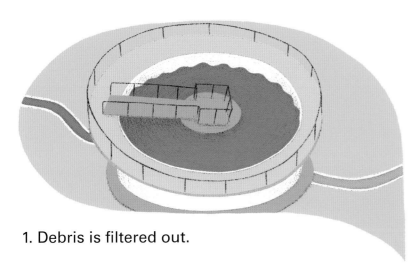

1. Debris is filtered out.

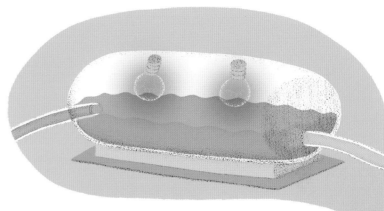

2. The water is disinfected, sometimes using ultraviolet light.

3. **Chlorine** is added to kill germs and reduce the risk of disease.

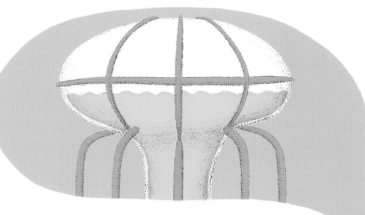

4. The water is safely stored in tanks before being carried through pipes to homes and businesses.

But clean drinking water can be contaminated again when it is used in the home. Think about the cleaning products you use to wash clothes and dishes or to take a shower. Would you drink a mouthful of water containing these products? Water that is perfectly drinkable when it comes out of the tap can quickly become undrinkable. It must be sent through a sewage system to the filtration treatment plant to go through the purification process all over again.

Water in Our Bodies

A camel can swallow the equivalent of a bathtub full of water and not need to drink again for a week. But it's different for people. We can go without food for a few weeks, but most humans will survive for only three to four days without water.

The human body is like a sponge. It must have water to work well. All the cells that make up the body need water—and lots of it. Our bodies are about 60 percent water, but our blood and our most important organs contain even more than that.

How Much Water Is in Our Organs?

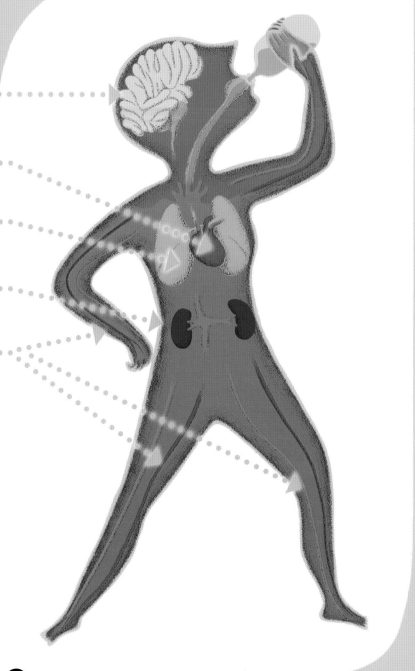

Brain	**73%**
Heart	**73%**
Lungs	**83%**
Kidneys	**79%**
Blood	**83%**

From birth until death, the average person will drink the equivalent of almost half an Olympic-sized swimming pool. And about 80 percent of the water you drink is absorbed and used by your body. The remaining 20 percent is excess and is released via your kidneys and bladder.

We Need Water

To stay healthy, we need water, both inside and out. Washing regularly with clean water is the best protection against diseases carried by bacteria and other **microorganisms**.

Many of us get the water that our bodies need from our household taps. But if this water is of poor quality, it can make us sick.

In the past, instead of washing off dirt, people scented their bodies with perfumes and powders to hide the smells. In 1850s France, most people took baths only about once every two years.

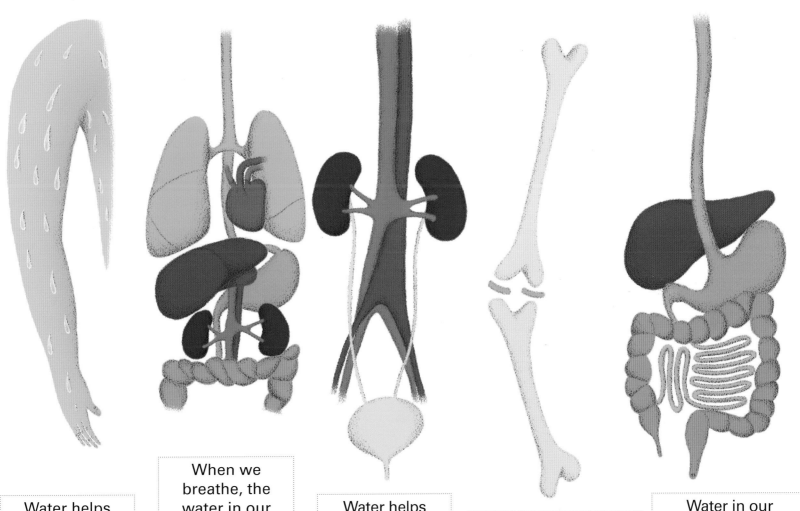

Water helps keep our bodies cool by absorbing heat and releasing it as sweat.

When we breathe, the water in our blood helps carry oxygen from the air in our lungs to all our organs.

Water helps clean out our bodies by carrying waste products in urine.

Water in the fluid between our bones helps to lubricate our joints so we can move them easily.

Water in our digestive system helps break down the food we eat so our bodies can absorb **nutrients**.

2. AIR

Like water, air is essential for living things, from humans to plants, fish, and insects. Air is a colorless and odorless mix of invisible gases.

What Is Air?

- 78% nitrogen

- 21% oxygen

- 1% other gases (including water vapor, argon, and carbon dioxide, plus fine particles such as dust, pollen, and ash)

Holding Your Breath

We need the oxygen in air to live. We can survive for four to six minutes without breathing, but after three minutes, our brain cells begin to stop functioning. The brain consumes more oxygen than any other organ.

Some divers can hold their breath for several minutes under water, but their bodies have adapted to allow them to do this without harm. They have more red blood cells and bigger lungs, and they take in extra oxygen before diving. The current world record for holding one's breath under water is twenty-four minutes!

Why Do We Need Air?

Humans

Humans, like all mammals, need to breathe in oxygen to turn the energy stored in our food into energy we can use to make our bodies work. The air we breathe in through our mouths and noses is carried to our lungs. There, the oxygen in the air is absorbed by our red blood cells and transported to all the cells of our bodies. Red blood cells carry carbon dioxide back to the lungs to be released when we exhale.

We aren't even aware of it, but every day 2,640 to 3,960 gallons (10,000 to 15,000 liters) of air circulates through our airways. That's enough air to fill a cement truck!

Marine Life

Marine mammals such as whales, seals, dolphins, and sea otters have respiratory systems similar to ours. They have to come to the surface of the water from time to time to breathe in air. Fish, on the other hand, can breathe under water. Instead of lungs, they have gills—thin tissues that extract oxygen from the water and circulate it in the blood.

Green Plants

Through photosynthesis, green plants transform the Sun's light energy into the sugar they need to grow. During this process, they absorb carbon dioxide from the air. After several chemical reactions take place, they release water and oxygen into the atmosphere. Without photosynthesis, there would be no green plants, and little food or **organic matter** for other creatures to eat.

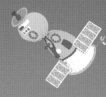

The Atmosphere

The atmosphere is a layer of gases that surrounds the Earth. Beyond the atmosphere is the vacuum of space.

Layers of the Atmosphere

- Troposphere (5 to 9 miles, or 8 to 14 kilometers, above Earth): This layer, which starts at the ground, is where clouds and weather develop; it's very thin, equivalent to the peel on an apple.

- Stratosphere (31 miles, or 50 kilometers): This is the location of the **ozone layer**, which protects us from the Sun's ultraviolet light.

- Mesosphere (53 miles, or 85 kilometers): The transition zone between the Earth and space, this is where meteorites burn up.

- Thermosphere (372 miles, or 600 kilometers): This is where the International Space Station orbits.

Why Do We Need the Atmosphere?

- It protects us from meteorites and the Sun's ultraviolet rays.

- It provides the oxygen that all living beings need.

- It provides plants with the carbon dioxide they need to grow.

- It keeps the Earth's surface warm.

- It reduces the temperature differences between night and day.

The auroras (northern and southern lights) are formed in the thermosphere when charged particles from the Sun hit the Earth's magnetic field, releasing energy that appears as bursts of light.

Atmospheric Pressure

Gravity holds the atmosphere close to the Earth, and the atmosphere puts weight on the surface of the planet and everything on it. This is called atmospheric pressure, and it is measured with an instrument called a **barometer**. As you climb higher in the atmosphere, the temperature cools and there is less air pressing down on you. The air pressure goes down.

Meteorologists speak of low pressure when the weather is cloudy or rainy. When the weather is dry, cloudless, and sunny, we are often in an area of high pressure.

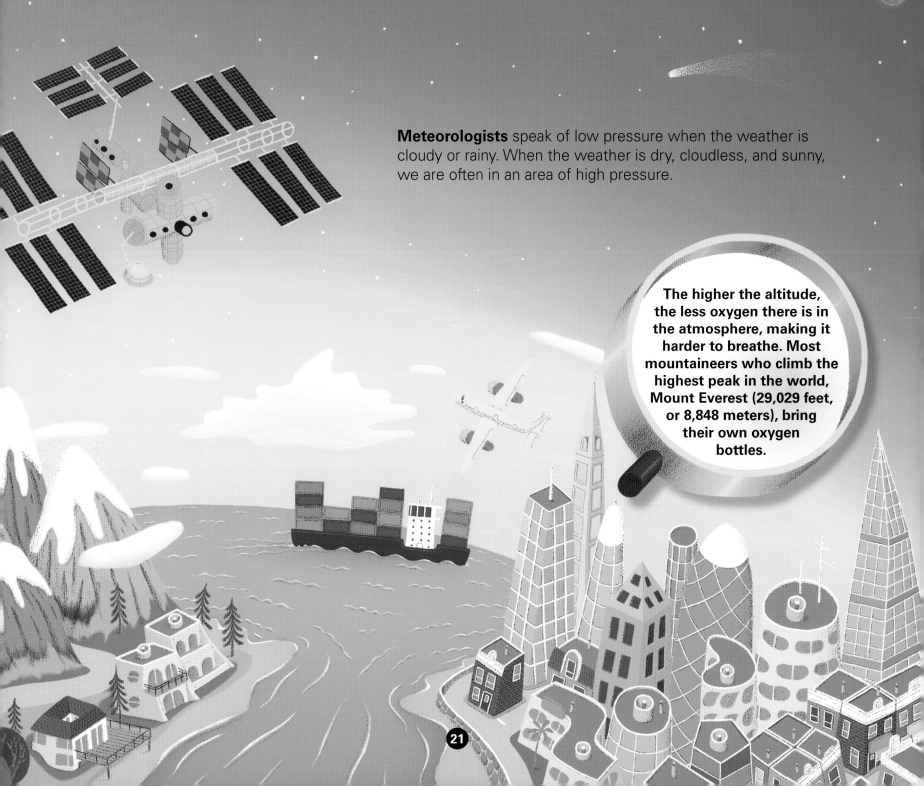

The higher the altitude, the less oxygen there is in the atmosphere, making it harder to breathe. Most mountaineers who climb the highest peak in the world, Mount Everest (29,029 feet, or 8,848 meters), bring their own oxygen bottles.

Wind

What Is Wind?

When the Sun heats up a mass of air, the air becomes lighter and rises. That creates an area of low pressure beneath it.

Cool air, such as the air at high altitudes, is heavier and it sinks. It exerts more downward pressure, creating an area of high pressure.

A difference in atmospheric pressure between two areas causes wind, as air always moves from the high- into the low-pressure area to balance out the pressure. We feel the moving air as wind. The greater the difference in temperature between the areas, the stronger the winds.

Wind is also affected by the rotation of the planet. And landforms such as mountains and valleys can influence airflow and cause regional winds.

The mistral and the tramontane are cold winds of the Mediterranean basin.

The hot and dry sirocco comes from the Sahara.

Chinooks are warm, moist air masses from the Pacific that blow over the Rocky Mountains, where they drop their moisture as snow or rain and then sweep down the eastern slopes as warm, dry winds.

Monsoons bring warm, humid air to South Asia and cause heavy rains.

Why Is Wind Important?

• It **oxygenates** the oceans by stirring up the water's surface in waves.

• It spreads seeds, spores, and pollen.

• It influences flying insect populations and bird migrations. Strong winds may discourage flying insects, a food source for some birds, from traveling. But winds in the right direction can help migrating birds by providing them with tailwinds.

The atmosphere on the moon is very thin, so there is no wind. The flag planted there by the Apollo 11 astronauts in 1969 is held out by a horizontal bar.

Jet streams are air currents in the upper atmosphere. They can lengthen or shorten long plane flights by as much as an hour, depending on whether the plane is flying with or against the current.

Cyclone or Tornado?

Some winds are so strong that they can cause serious and even devastating damage.

A cyclone is formed in an area of low atmospheric pressure. The air moves upward from near an ocean's surface, creating violent winds. Typhoons, hurricanes, and tropical cyclones are different names for the same phenomenon. The name varies depending on where in the world the event takes place.

A tornado is a violently spinning column of air from a thunderstorm that stretches down to the ground. A tornado's destructive power is enormous.

The United States has more tornadoes than any other country in the world—about a thousand every year.

Threats to Air Quality

A pollutant is anything that has a negative effect on the quality of the atmosphere. Air pollution occurs when particles and gases in the air reach levels that are harmful enough to affect the world's climate, as well as the health of living things.

Air pollution can be caused by both natural phenomena and human activity. Dust, pollen, smoke, and gases like carbon dioxide can all be sources of air pollution. Because the atmosphere doesn't respect borders, pollutants can travel long distances, from one country to another.

Air Pollution Caused by Natural Phenomena

• Volcanic eruptions spew ash and sulfur dioxide.

• Smoke from forest fires carries fine particles over long distances.

• Flowers release high concentrations of pollen.

• Organic decomposition produces **methane** (a gas released from wetlands and the digestive tracts of animals).

Air Pollution Caused by Human Activity

Outside
• Industrial smokestacks

• Agricultural activity (pesticides, fertilizers, burning of waste)

• Exhaust fumes from fuel combustion in motor vehicles

• Generating power for heating and air-conditioning

• Waste treatment facilities (incinerators)

Chemical pollutants from the burning of fossil fuels (such as oil, natural gas, and coal) have the biggest effect on the quality of outdoor air.

Inside
• Household cleaning products

• Certain household fragrances (such as scented candles and air fresheners)

• Cosmetics

• Paints, varnishes, and craft products

It may seem surprising, but indoor air can be as polluted as outdoor air. Renovations (painting, sanding, varnishing), cooking, and housecleaning can all pollute our homes, releasing dust, particles, and fibers that remain suspended in the air.

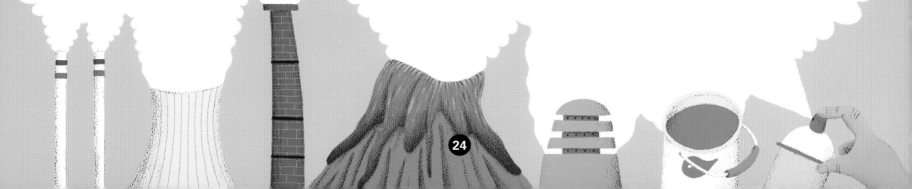

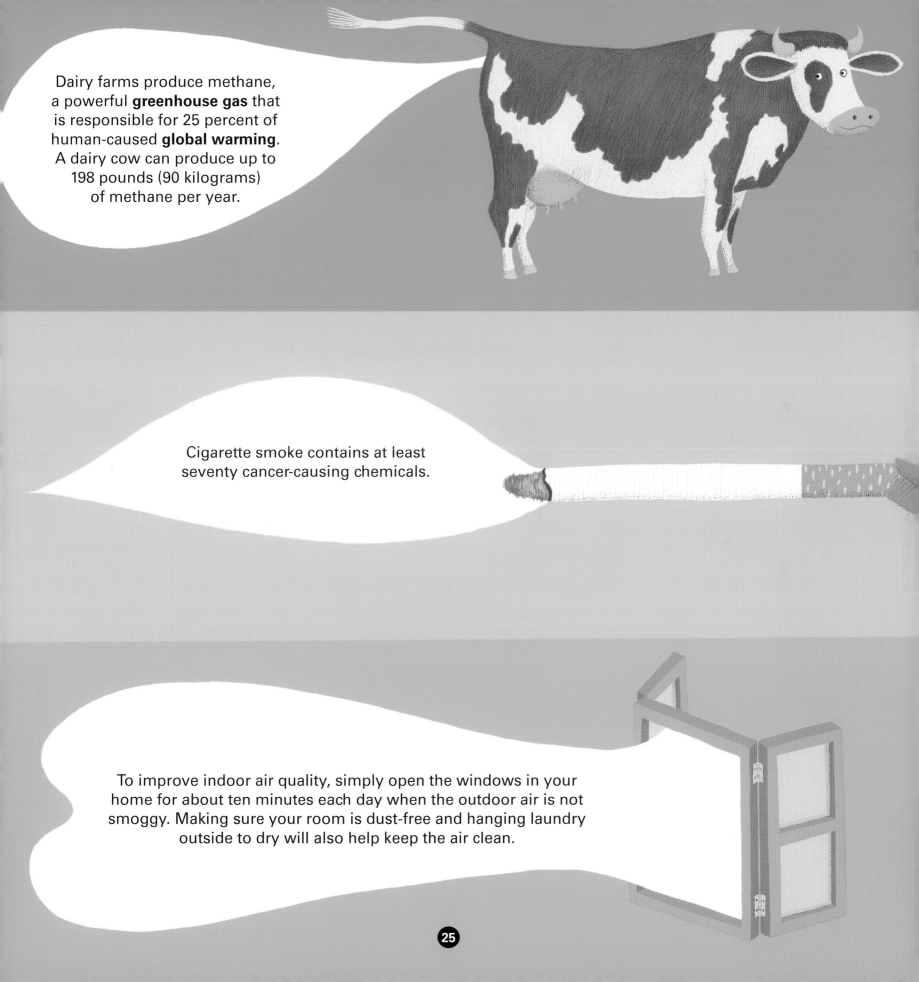

Dairy farms produce methane, a powerful **greenhouse gas** that is responsible for 25 percent of human-caused **global warming**. A dairy cow can produce up to 198 pounds (90 kilograms) of methane per year.

Cigarette smoke contains at least seventy cancer-causing chemicals.

To improve indoor air quality, simply open the windows in your home for about ten minutes each day when the outdoor air is not smoggy. Making sure your room is dust-free and hanging laundry outside to dry will also help keep the air clean.

Effects of Air Pollution

On Humans

Over time, exposure to contaminated air can affect human health.

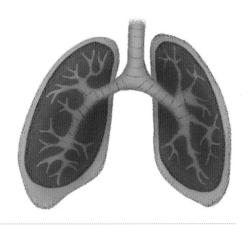

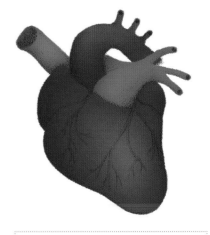

Pollution attacks the airways and lungs and can cause asthma, allergies, and respiratory diseases. It can also increase the risk of cancer.

Pollution attacks the eyes and skin, resulting in conjunctivitis, skin disorders, and an increase in the risk of cancer.

Pollution can affect the cardiovascular system, introducing very fine particles into the blood.

On Plants and Animals

Pollutants can affect plants and animals in different ways.

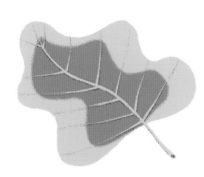

Fine particles can clog the pores of leaves and slow down photosynthesis.

Acid rain damages leaves and seeps into the ground, destroying microorganisms that keep the soil healthy. Acidic soil also makes trees more vulnerable to pests and disease.

Air pollution also affects certain animal species, such as honeybees, which pollinate 80 percent of the world's food crops. Air pollution interferes with the bees' ability to follow flower scents.

On the Planet

Heat from the Sun penetrates the lower layers of the atmosphere. Gases such as carbon dioxide trap some of this heat, creating the **greenhouse effect**, a natural process that keeps the planet warm enough to sustain life. But when too many greenhouse gases are produced, they become pollutants, causing the atmosphere to heat up unnaturally quickly. We call this global warming. This warming is causing the Earth's climate to change.

What about Ozone?

Artificial chemicals called chlorofluorocarbons (CFCs) have been used to make refrigerators, air conditioners, and aerosol containers. These chemicals floated into the upper atmosphere, where they helped create a hole in the ozone layer, which protects us from the Sun's ultraviolet light. In 1987, many countries agreed to limit the use of CFCs. Without this joint action, the ozone hole would be much, much bigger today. Instead, it is expected to heal completely by 2060.

Without the greenhouse effect, the Earth's surface temperature would be −0.4°F (−18°C)—too cold for life as we know it.

How Can We Improve Air Quality?

Around the world, cities and countries are taking measures to reduce carbon dioxide emissions and lessen the effects of global warming:

• Building bike lanes, improving public transit systems, encouraging carpooling, and developing pedestrian-only streets to limit the number of vehicles in city cores

• Composting rather than burning organic waste

• Constructing eco-friendly buildings that use less energy to heat, cool, and build

• Using vehicles powered by clean energy

• Installing green spaces such as parks, green roofs, and vertical gardens to absorb carbon dioxide, filter out pollutants, and keep areas cool

3. SOIL

**Soil is the uppermost part of the Earth's surface.
But what goes on in this thin layer (on average just
12 inches or 30 centimeters thick) that surrounds our planet?**

Soil is essential to the survival of most living things. It's a mixture of rock particles (from large rocks to grains of sand), clay, and bits of dead plants and animals. Air and water circulate through soil, which teems with all kinds of life-forms, from mice and earthworms to plants, bacteria, and fungi. Soil holds the roots of trees and plants, keeping them stable. It helps regulate the climate by absorbing and releasing gases, water vapor, and dust. It also cleans the water that runs through it.

It can take hundreds or even thousands of years for soil to form. Wind, erosion, and the presence or absence of plants and microorganisms all contribute to its makeup.

What Is Soil?

Soil is composed of four elements:

1. Water runs through it and carries oxygen, carbon dioxide, and mineral salts.

2. Air allows the exchange of carbon and oxygen between the soil and the atmosphere.

3. Minerals define the texture of the soil (sand, **silt**, or clay).

4. Organic matter, or the decaying remains of living things, makes up **humus**.

The lives of seven billion people and an untold number of species depend on the health of this top layer of the Earth's surface.

Earthworms help with soil formation:

- By digging tunnels in the ground, they allow water to penetrate and drain more easily.

- They **aerate** the soil, allowing oxygen to enter and carbon dioxide to escape.

- They help fertilize the soil by eating decomposing plant matter, which they then excrete on the surface. This removes contaminants and adds nutrients to the earth.

An earthworm can digest up to 40 tons (36 tonnes) of soil a year. That's like eating six elephants!

Earthworms are also used to produce compost. This is called **vermiculture**.

How Soil Is Formed

Soil is formed in a slow process that happens in two main stages:

Stage 1: The top layer of the Earth's crust, called bedrock, is slowly destroyed by water runoff, wind, and freezing and thawing. This accumulated rock and mineral debris is the basis of soil.

Stage 2: Gradually, this soil layer is enriched with organic material, like dead leaves, roots, and bark. Bacteria, fungi, and **invertebrates** help transform this material into humus, which is essential for plant development.

Soil Layers

Surface litter
is a mix of dead leaves and decaying plants. It serves as a hiding place or home for small animals.

Humus
is created when the surface litter decomposes.

Topsoil
is cultivable and good for supporting life. It's a mixture rich in humus and minerals.

Bedrock
is the rocky top layer of the Earth's crust.

Types of Soil

All soils are not the same. The soil's texture depends on its proportions of sand, silt, and clay. A soil is well structured when the particles of sand and silt are bound in small clumps by clay, humus, and calcium, allowing air and water to move through.

Sandy Soil
Made mostly of sand, this soil has a granular texture.
It doesn't hold water and dries out quickly.

Silty Soil
Composed mainly of silt (accumulated earth deposited on the banks of a river or lake),
this soil is smooth in texture. Its particles can break down into small pieces.

Clay Soil
Mainly composed of clay minerals, this is a heavy,
dense soil with a sticky texture.

Humus-Bearing Soil
Mainly composed of organic material, this soil can retain large
amounts of water without becoming compacted.

The Role of Soil

- It allows the production of food, fuel, fibers, and other materials needed for human activities.

- It filters and cleans the water that runs through it to replenish groundwater reserves.

- It helps control floods by absorbing and holding back water.

- It removes and stores carbon from the air, which lowers carbon dioxide levels in the atmosphere.

- It provides a habitat for several thousand species of animals, plants, and microorganisms.

- It holds the memory of human civilizations by preserving buried objects from the past.

- It provides a foundation for buildings and roads.

- It forms features of the landscape.

A billion microorganisms can be found in a single teaspoon of soil, representing up to ten thousand different species.

Threats to Soil

Soils have formed over tens of thousands of years. But it has taken only a few hundred years of human activity to pollute them.

Human activity has degraded the quality of the soil in a number of ways:

- Deforestation and the destruction of hedges, ditches, and embankments have caused soil erosion. Off-road leisure activities such as mountain biking, ATVs, and motocross have added to the problem.

- Cultivable soils are being overused, which prevents them from replenishing their nutrients.

- Heavy machinery squeezes out air and water, compacting the soil.

- The spread of cities and roads has resulted in the loss of natural areas.

- Rain forests have been burned to make room for farmland, depleting soil nutrients and making soils susceptible to erosion without roots to hold them in place.

Soil microorganisms such as bacteria and fungi can help break down pollutants caused by human activities.

Soil Pollution

Many types of pollutants settle into the soil, affecting the plants and animals that live there.

- Industrial oils, heavy metals, detergents, hydrocarbons, solvents, varnishes, and paints

- Chemicals such as fertilizers, insecticides, and herbicides

- Solid nonorganic waste that has been dumped and not disposed of properly, including old appliances, furniture, tires, and mattresses

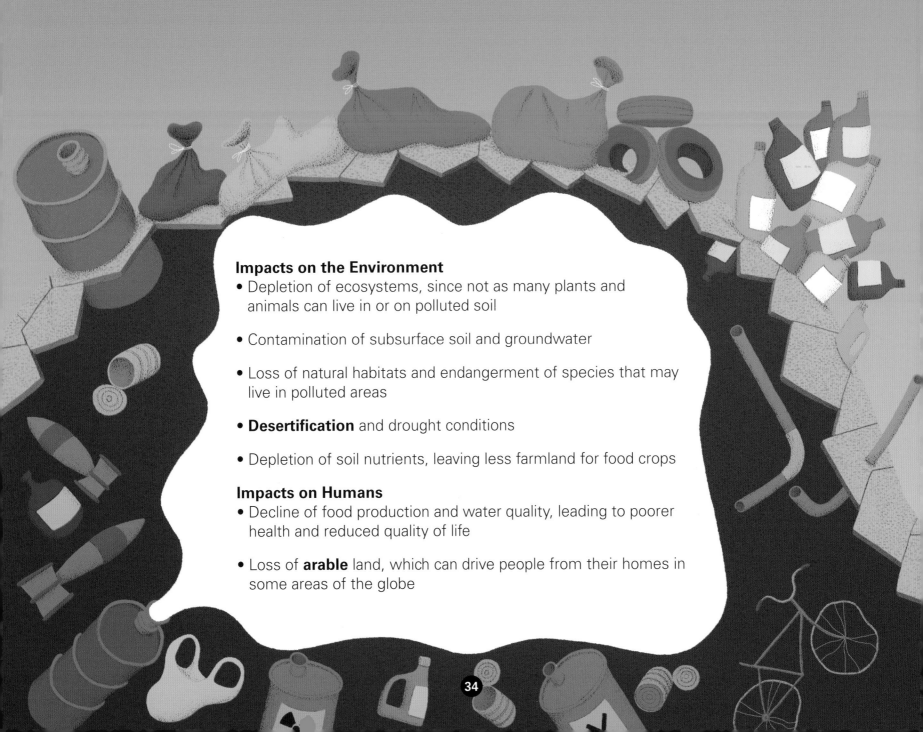

Impacts on the Environment
- Depletion of ecosystems, since not as many plants and animals can live in or on polluted soil

- Contamination of subsurface soil and groundwater

- Loss of natural habitats and endangerment of species that may live in polluted areas

- **Desertification** and drought conditions

- Depletion of soil nutrients, leaving less farmland for food crops

Impacts on Humans
- Decline of food production and water quality, leading to poorer health and reduced quality of life

- Loss of **arable** land, which can drive people from their homes in some areas of the globe

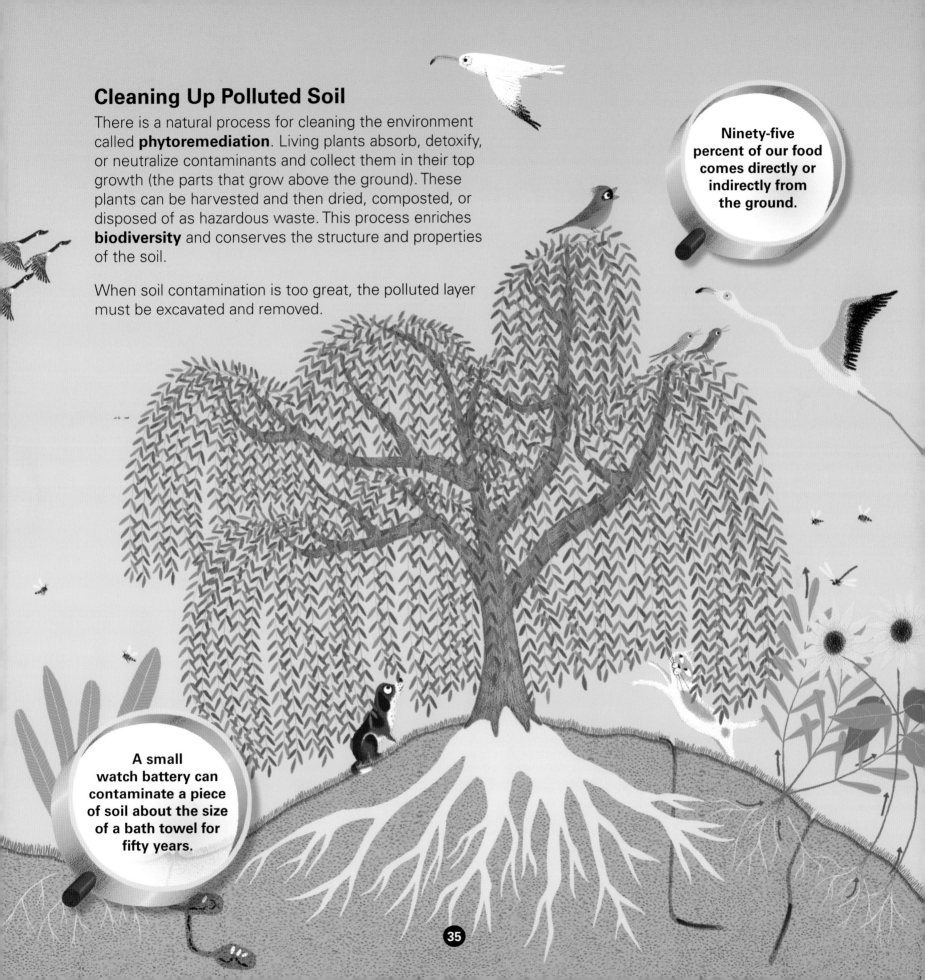

Cleaning Up Polluted Soil

There is a natural process for cleaning the environment called **phytoremediation**. Living plants absorb, detoxify, or neutralize contaminants and collect them in their top growth (the parts that grow above the ground). These plants can be harvested and then dried, composted, or disposed of as hazardous waste. This process enriches **biodiversity** and conserves the structure and properties of the soil.

When soil contamination is too great, the polluted layer must be excavated and removed.

Ninety-five percent of our food comes directly or indirectly from the ground.

A small watch battery can contaminate a piece of soil about the size of a bath towel for fifty years.

4. ENERGY

Energy is what allows us to work, move, and eat. We need energy to carry out all the activities of our daily lives. For example, kicking a ball requires energy. Without the force of a kicking foot, the ball will not move.

We eat food to accumulate the energy that allows our muscles and other body parts to accomplish different tasks. But energy comes from many sources. Cars get energy from gasoline. Lights get energy from electricity. Some homes are heated with energy that's captured from deep underground.

And the more people there are on the planet, the more energy we need.

In 1950, there were 2.5 billion people in the world. There were 7.7 billion in 2019. And the population keeps growing. Each year, it increases by another 80 million people.

It takes about 4 gallons (15 liters) of oil to make a pair of jeans and transport them to a store.

Why We Need Energy

When humans learned how to make fire, wood became their main energy source. They burned it to keep themselves warm, cook their food, and scare off wild animals.

Today the world guzzles energy. The more people there are, the more things we do, the more items we make, and the more energy we use.

We need energy for

- Transportation

- Heating and lighting our homes

- Powering our computers, TVs, and other electronic devices

- Keeping ourselves housed, fed, and clothed

- Growing the food we consume

- Constructing and maintaining our buildings, roads, and railways

- Providing services such as health, education, and transportation

Where Does Energy Come From?

Renewable Energy

Renewable energy comes from natural resources that are constantly being replenished, which means they cannot be used up. Using renewable energy in place of burning fossil fuels reduces the amount of carbon dioxide we produce.

Sun
- Solar thermal energy uses solar cells to convert sunlight into heat, which can warm a house or a tank of water.

- Solar photovoltaic energy uses solar panels to convert sunlight into electricity.

Wind
- Wind energy uses wind power to turn **turbine** blades and produce electricity.

Water
- Hydro power uses tides, waves, currents, waterfalls, and dams to generate electricity from moving water.

Biomass
- Biomass energy uses organic materials such as plants and animal waste as fuel.

Geothermal
- Geothermal energy draws heat from the ground and underground hot springs.

The center of the Earth holds an immense amount of heat. Its temperature is around 11,700°F (6,500°C).

Energy from Fossil Fuels

Fossil fuels come from organic matter that has been decomposing in the ground for several million years. These fuels contain carbon, which is released into the atmosphere as carbon dioxide when they're burned.

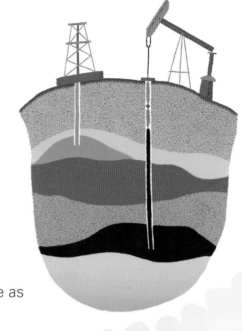

- Oil and natural gas are formed from decomposing plants and animals. Burning natural gas produces less carbon dioxide than burning oil or coal. The gas is often extracted from the ground by a process called **fracking**, which releases methane, a powerful greenhouse gas, into the atmosphere.

- Coal is formed from ancient swamp plants and trees that were buried and compressed over time. Burning coal produces almost twice as much carbon dioxide as burning natural gas.

We call fossil fuels nonrenewable resources because they take millions of years to form.

Nuclear Energy

Nuclear energy is produced by splitting atoms in a reactor to create heat. The waste from this process is **radioactive** and can be dangerous if not properly stored.

The Earth's Energy Challenges

Reducing greenhouse gases is one of the major challenges of **sustainable development**. To achieve this, we must make some changes:

- Increase our use of renewable energies and develop the means to store them.

- Reduce our energy consumption by promoting the use of public transportation, recycling waste, and making our homes and behaviors as energy efficient as possible.

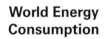

World Energy Consumption

- Oil—32.5%
- Coal—27.9%
- Natural gas—23.4%
- Renewable energy sources— 11.8%
- Nuclear energy—4.4%

5. CLIMATE

Climate is the prevailing weather conditions in an area over a long period of time. Climatology is the study of long-term climate conditions. Meteorology focuses on short-term weather conditions that occur day to day.

To define a climate, scientists observe and analyze atmospheric conditions in a given geographical area over a long period of time (twenty to thirty years). They study several phenomena:

- Temperature

- Humidity

- Atmospheric pressure

- Amount and type of precipitation (rain, snow, etc.)

- Wind

- Quantity and quality of clouds

All this information is averaged to determine the planet's climate zones.

What Are Earth's Climate Zones?

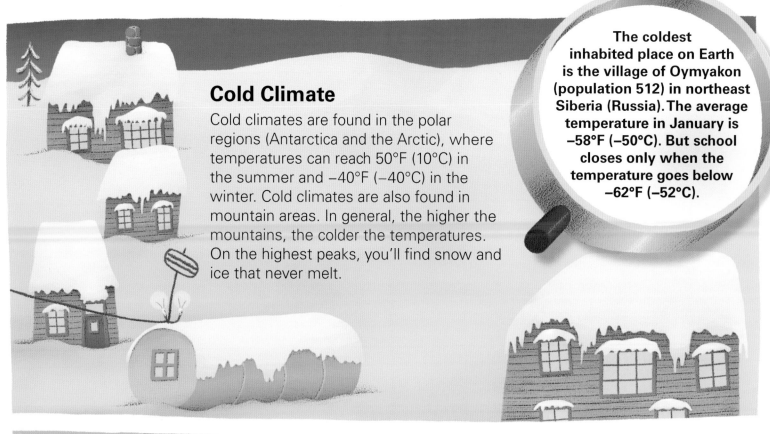

Cold Climate

Cold climates are found in the polar regions (Antarctica and the Arctic), where temperatures can reach 50°F (10°C) in the summer and −40°F (−40°C) in the winter. Cold climates are also found in mountain areas. In general, the higher the mountains, the colder the temperatures. On the highest peaks, you'll find snow and ice that never melt.

The coldest inhabited place on Earth is the village of Oymyakon (population 512) in northeast Siberia (Russia). The average temperature in January is −58°F (−50°C). But school closes only when the temperature goes below −62°F (−52°C).

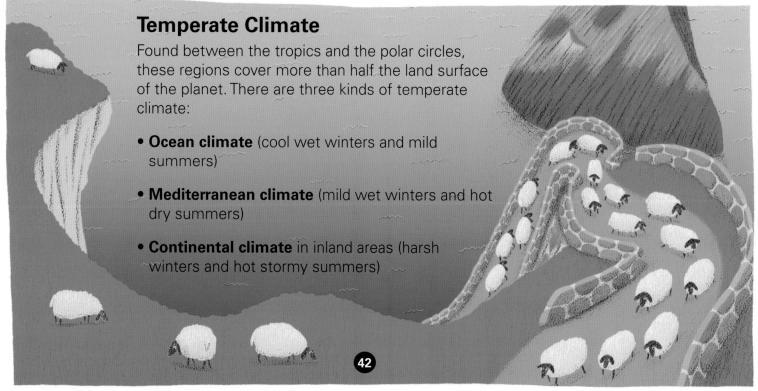

Temperate Climate

Found between the tropics and the polar circles, these regions cover more than half the land surface of the planet. There are three kinds of temperate climate:

- **Ocean climate** (cool wet winters and mild summers)

- **Mediterranean climate** (mild wet winters and hot dry summers)

- **Continental climate** in inland areas (harsh winters and hot stormy summers)

Tropical Climate

Found in areas near the equator, between the tropics, this climate has very hot temperatures. Some regions receive abundant rains, while others are drier.

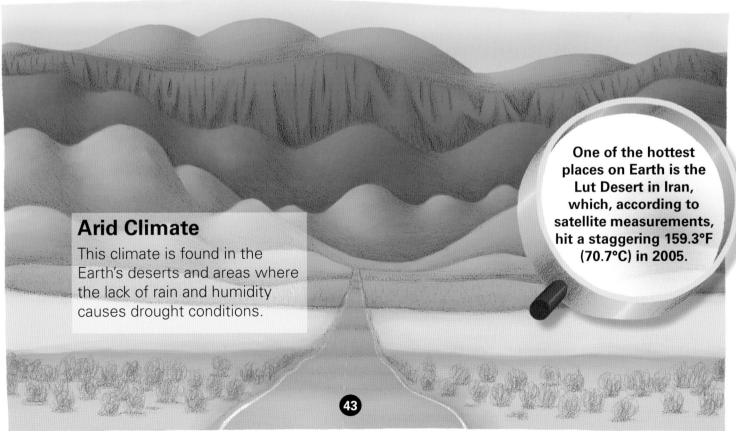

Arid Climate

This climate is found in the Earth's deserts and areas where the lack of rain and humidity causes drought conditions.

One of the hottest places on Earth is the Lut Desert in Iran, which, according to satellite measurements, hit a staggering 159.3°F (70.7°C) in 2005.

Influences on the Climate

The Earth's climates depend on three phenomena.

Amount of sunlight

The Sun's radiation, or light, strikes the atmosphere that surrounds the planet. Part of this radiation is reflected back into space, but the rest passes through the atmosphere to Earth.

Distribution of the Sun's energy

Even once this radiation has passed through the atmosphere, not all of it remains. Some of it is reflected back into space—especially by white surfaces like ice and snow. But some is absorbed by the Earth's surface. This absorbed energy is released as heat.

Greenhouse effect

In a greenhouse, sunlight passes through the glass or plastic walls and roof and is absorbed by the plants and the soil inside, which give off heat. The greenhouse glass prevents that heat from escaping and keeps the inside warm. The same thing happens with the planet. Sunlight passes through the transparent atmosphere and is absorbed by the Earth's surface and converted into heat. Gases in the atmosphere trap this heat and send it back down to Earth. This is how the planet is warmed.

The main greenhouse gases are water vapor, carbon dioxide, methane, and nitrous oxide.

Our eyes can see only a small part of the Sun's light. This visible light appears to us as the colors of the spectrum, from red to violet. But beyond this spectrum there is ultraviolet light and infrared light, which we can't see. Ultraviolet light can kill bacteria, but it can also damage living plant and animal tissue and cause sunburns. Hot objects radiate infrared light, which we can feel as heat. We can see infrared light with special cameras.

A layer of ozone in the upper atmosphere absorbs ultraviolet light and prevents most of it from reaching the Earth.

Climate Change

Over the course of its long history, the Earth has gone through many gradual climate changes, reaching temperatures much colder or hotter than those we are experiencing today. And the Earth's atmosphere has always acted like a kind of blanket, with the greenhouse effect keeping the planet warm enough to sustain life.

But unnaturally high levels of methane and carbon dioxide are now building up in the atmosphere. The rapid increase in these greenhouse gases is causing climate change. The gases are being produced by human activities, and they are forming a denser and denser layer around the Earth, trapping more heat that would normally escape back into space. This adds to the natural greenhouse effect and causes surface temperatures to rise. This is the phenomenon called global warming.

By analyzing ice layers in Antarctica and Greenland, scientists can see how temperatures and the composition of gases in the atmosphere have changed over thousands of years.

Causes of Global Warming

Human activities related to industrialization and our modern lifestyles are largely responsible for the rapid rise in greenhouse gas emissions. These gases come mainly from burning fossil fuels in industry and transportation, but there are other sources:

- **Deforestation of large tropical forests**—Forests absorb carbon dioxide from the atmosphere and hold it in their leaves and bark; it's also stored in the soil. The gas is released back into the air when the trees are burned.

- **Intensive agriculture**—Fertilizers release nitrous oxide, and large livestock farms emit methane.

- **Air travel**—The exhaust from jet planes releases carbon into the atmosphere. This exhaust also remains in the cooler upper atmosphere for several hours, trapping heat that would normally escape.

- **Melting permafrost**—As the Earth's surface warms, ancient frozen swamps are melting for the first time since the last ice age, releasing methane, a powerful greenhouse gas.

Effects of Global Warming

Scientists have been warning us about climate change for more than thirty years. If nothing is done to limit greenhouse gas emissions, the Earth's temperature will continue to rise.

Global Warming Is Already Affecting the Planet …

- Rising sea levels threaten some low-lying islands and coastal areas.

- As the oceans pull more carbon dioxide from the atmosphere, **acidification** is occurring, making it harder for corals and shellfish to build their skeletons and shells.

- Extreme weather events, including torrential rains, hurricanes, and floods, grow more common as a warmer atmosphere holds more moisture.

- Desert areas expand as the land surface heats up.

- Some species die out or are forced to move to new habitats as areas grow too warm.

... And Our Daily Lives

• Global warming affects some areas of the world more than others. In countries near the equator, for example, dry zones could receive even less rain, increasing the risk of famine and forcing large numbers of people to migrate in search of food.

• Changes in climate affect which plants can be grown where. In some regions, it may become impossible to grow crops that have been farmed there for generations, upsetting the lives of the people and industries that depend on them.

• Disease-carrying species like mosquitoes and ticks move with the warmer climate into new areas, bringing infectious illnesses such as malaria and Lyme disease.

• Extreme weather events increase the risks to human health. Heat waves cause respiratory problems and put special stress on children, the poor, and the elderly.

THE FUTURE

"The path is made by walking." —Antonio Machado, Spanish poet

Some cultures refer to our planet as Mother Earth, because the Earth gives us life and nourishes all living things. Yet many people don't seem to care that over time we have created an environment that is no longer healthy. Fortunately, other people are realizing that this is the only home we have.

In the late 1990s, Sebastião Salgado, a famous photographer, went back to the Brazilian rain-forest farm where he grew up. But he was sad to see that because of deforestation and drought, all the vegetation of his valley and hills had disappeared. No more birds, no more animals. Nothing but a vast expanse of dust.

"What if we replant the forest?" his wife, Lélia, said.

Twenty years later, more than two million trees have been planted, and birds and other animals—many that are endangered—have returned.

Every day, people across the globe are taking action to solve our environmental challenges—improving air quality, developing renewable energies, and growing food without using chemical fertilizers or pesticides. And every act—from the tiny to the seemingly impossible—is needed.

Cities, such as Vancouver, B.C., are creating parks and planting urban forests. These green spaces reduce the effect of heat islands—urban areas where lots of people, vehicles, and buildings share a small space, generating energy and heat and making the area warmer than the surrounding countryside.

In the Philippines, people are using solar energy to turn plastic bottles into light bulbs. A bottle filled with water and a small amount of bleach (to prevent bacteria growth) is inserted into a hole cut in a corrugated metal roof. The water in the bottle changes the angle of the sunlight to light up the room below. It's an innovative way to bring light to poorer areas of the country.

The small Swedish town of Växjö uses and distributes energy derived from biomass—wood waste from the forest industry—to heat its buildings. Its city buses run on biogas from food waste, and there are roughly 56 miles (90 kilometers) of bike trails in the area.

People in Detroit, Michigan, are transforming vacant spaces into urban farms and gardens, which provide local, healthy food, jobs, and a growing sense of community in a city with high levels of poverty and food scarcity.

It's not the size of the gesture that's important. It's understanding why it's necessary and then choosing to do it. We can build a better future for everyone if we all do what we can. Pack a reusable water bottle or straw. Ride your bike to school. Plant a tree. Or use bruised fruit to make a smoothie. These may seem like small actions, yet multiplied by millions of people, they are a way to keep our planet healthy and well.

If we take care of the Earth, it will also look after us.

GLOSSARY

acid rain. A mix of rain and polluting gases from vehicles and factory smoke.

acidification. Chemical changes that take place in water, air, or soil, increasing their acidity. This phenomenon seriously harms the environment.

aerate. To supply the soil with air. Aeration helps organic matter decompose, which enriches the soil.

aquaculture. The farming of fish, crustaceans, mollusks, or seaweed in a closed breeding area, such as a pond or a river.

arable. Land that is suitable for farming.

bacteria (bacterium, singular). Single-celled organisms invisible to the naked eye. Bacteria are found everywhere on Earth, including in the human body.

barometer. An instrument for measuring atmospheric pressure.

biodiversity. All of the living organisms on Earth or in a given environment.

chlorine. A chemical used as a disinfectant for purifying water.

climate change. Any change in the Earth's weather patterns. Human activities are currently causing climate change through global warming.

desertification. An irreversible change in which fertile land becomes desert.

ecosystem. A community of interacting living and nonliving things in a particular physical environment.

excrement. Waste matter from humans or animals.

fracking. The process of injecting fluid into underground rocks so that the oil or natural gas trapped there can flow out and up to the surface through a pipe.

global warming. An increase in Earth's average temperatures caused by the greenhouse effect. Global warming is one aspect of climate change.

greenhouse effect. A natural phenomenon that warms Earth's lower atmosphere and ensures a livable temperature for the planet. Increased levels of carbon dioxide and other pollutants have strengthened the greenhouse effect, causing global warming.

greenhouse gas. Any gas that absorbs infrared radiation and traps heat in the atmosphere. Greenhouse gases cause the greenhouse effect.

groundwater. A reserve of water found in wells, springs, aquifers, and other places under the Earth's surface.

herbicide. A substance used to destroy unwanted or invasive plants.

humus. Decomposed plant or animal matter that enriches the soil with carbon and minerals.

industrial revolution. A period of history in the late 1700s and early 1800s marked by the rapid introduction of machinery.

invertebrate. An animal that does not have a spine.

meteorologist. Someone who works in the field of meteorology.

meteorology. A science dedicated to the study of weather (temperature, precipitation, winds, etc.).

methane. A powerful greenhouse gas that is colorless and odorless. It's produced mainly by animals such as cattle and sheep, and by wetlands such as swamps.

microorganism. A living organism invisible to the naked eye.

nutrient. A substance that provides nourishment to living things.

organic matter. Any material in soil that contains carbon and comes from plants and animals or their waste products. Decomposing organic matter produces humus.

oxygenate. To supply a fluid or other substance, such as the blood, with oxygen.

ozone layer. A layer of the atmosphere that absorbs most of the ultraviolet radiation from the Sun.

photosynthesis. The process by which green plants transform carbon dioxide and water into nutrients using energy from sunlight.

phytoplankton. Tiny plant species that drift with the ocean currents.

phytoremediation. A process that uses plants to remove toxic substances from polluted land, water, or air.

potable. Water that's safe to drink.

radioactive. Can emit energy or particles.

silt. Accumulated earth deposited on the banks of a river or lake.

sustainable development. An approach to economic and social development that meets the needs of current human activities without compromising the quality of natural resources for future generations.

turbine. An engine that uses water or air to turn its blades to create energy.

vermiculture. The cultivation of worms, especially for use in composting.

SELECTED SOURCES

The English-language edition of this book was created in consultation with Dr. Virginia Capmourteres, School of Environmental Sciences, University of Guelph.

"Air Travel and Climate Change." David Suzuki Foundation, 5 Oct. 2017. Online.

"Benefits of Renewable Energy Use." Union of Concerned Scientists, Science for a Healthy Planet and Safer World, 20 Dec. 2017. Online.

Boysen, Margret. *Alice au pays du climat*. Paris: Le Pommier, 2018.

Bréon, François-Marie and Gilles Luneau. *Atlas du climat: Face aux défis du réchauffement*. Paris: Autrement, 2018.

Creimer, Diego and Louise Hénault-Éthier, Karel Mayrand, Julie Roy. *Demain, le Québec: Des initiatives inspirantes pour un monde plus vert et plus juste*. Montréal: La Presse, 2018.

Davison, Devita. "How urban agriculture is transforming Detroit." TED, April 2017.

"Earth's Atmospheric Layers." National Aeronautics and Space Administration, 22 Jan. 2013. Online.

"Facts and Statistics: Did You Know?" Safe Drinking Water Foundation, 23 Jan. 2017. Online.

Funk, McKenzie. "Sebastião Salgado Has Seen the Forest, Now He's Seeing the Trees." *Smithsonian Magazine*, October 2015. Online.

"The Great Pacific Garbage Patch." The Ocean Cleanup, 2019. Online.

Herring, Peg. "The secret life of soil." OSU Extension Service, Oregon State University. Online.

Hunt, Ellie. "38 million pieces of plastic waste found on uninhabited South Pacific island." *The Guardian*, 15 May 2017. Online.

"Ice, Snow, and Glaciers and the Water Cycle." Water Science School, U.S. Geological Survey. Online.

Jancovici, Jean-Marc. *Le changeiment climatique expliqué à ma fille*. Paris: Seuil, 2017.

Kandel, Robert. *Le réchauffement climatique*. Paris: PUF, 2010.

Levallois, Patrick et Pierre Lajoie, éds. *Air intérieur et eau potable. Environnement et santé*. Paris: PUF, 1990.

Lin, Kevin. "Seasonal Science: What Lurks in the Leaf Litter?" *Scientific American*, October 2012. Online.

Live Science Staff. "Where's the Hottest Place on Earth?" Live Science, 16 Apr. 2012. Online.

"Ocean Acidification." *National Geographic*. 27 Apr. 2017. Online.

Orendain, Simone. "In Philippine Slums, Capturing Light in a Bottle." *All Things Considered*, NPR, 28 Dec. 2011.

Pfleger, Paige. "Detroit's Urban Farms: Engines of Growth, Omens of Change." *The Pulse*, WHYY, 11 Jan. 2018. Online.

"Severe Weather 101: Tornado Basics." The National Severe Storms Laboratory, National Oceanic and Atmospheric Administration. Online.

"The Water in You: Water and the Human Body." Water Science School, U.S. Geological Survey. Online.

Vernier, Jacques. *Les énergies renouvelables.* Paris: PUF, 2017.

"What Causes Wind to Blow?" YouTube, uploaded by Met Office, 24 Apr. 2017.

"Where is all of the Earth's Water?" National Ocean Service, National Oceanic and Atmospheric Administration. Online.

Zolfagharifard, Ellie. "Watch cargo ships sail Earth's oceans: Hypnotic interactive map follows the route of giant vessels over a year." *Daily Mail*, 27 Apr. 2016. Online.

INDEX

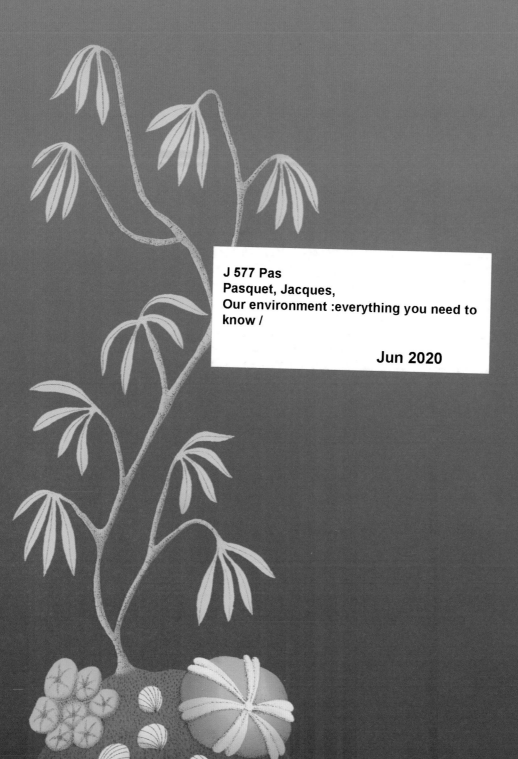